MORE THAN
PEACE,
POWER &
PRESENCE
THROUGH
MEDITATION

MORE THAN
PEACE, POWER & PRESENCE
THROUGH
MEDITATION

gatekeeper press™

Columbus, Ohio

More than Peace, Power & Presence through Meditation

Published by Gatekeeper Press
2167 Stringtown Rd, Suite 109
Columbus, OH 43123-2989
www.GatekeeperPress.com

Library of Congress Control Number: 2020946857

ISBN (paperback): 978-1-66290-502-5
eISBN: 978-1-66290-503-2

CONTENTS

INTRODUCTION

Human beings have always been very judgmental, but easy access to social media makes it seem as if there is a lot more judgment today. There are all kinds pro and anti groups—Pro-choice and Anti-choice; Black Lives Matter versus All Lives Matter; Pro-Trump versus Anti-Trump, etc. There is no conversation between the two sides, and each side is very sure that the other side is bad and to be judged as bad. We usually get triggered by actions of others that we refuse to see in ourselves. See if you can test the truth of that statement. The next time you find yourself judging someone, try taking a deep breath, and then put your hand on your heart and ask yourself if there is any action you take that is close to the action you are judging. I realized this a few years ago when I noticed that as I railed against violence in the world, my thoughts about people who had different political opinions were violent, and my instinct was to swat them off like flies.

The instinct was to extinguish their opinion. As a person who calls herself left of liberal, I recognized that I could hate as the best of those whom I judged for hating, I can be as bitter and angry and I can be as judgmental. It took me a minute to accept the fact that I was as flawed as the person I judged. Then, using the techniques described in the book here, I learned to open my heart to myself and accept me with all my flaws.

What happens when we open the door to all our flaws and look them square in the face? You become a human being who is completely comfortable in your skin. You do not suppress and hide any part of you. You welcome your light and shadow. As a result, you become a more integrated human being who does not need to judge others to feel good about yourself. As I often tell my clients, this journey towards complete integration is not linear. It is the work of a lifetime. However, even a few steps along the path result in a greater peace, more focus, and a lot more compassion for the struggles of other human beings along the path. This increased peace with who you are is reflected in your energy and the work you put out into the world. This is why I am so passionate about encouraging you to do the work in this book. I believe with all my heart that, as you do this work of integration, you radiate the increased peace within you, into your immediate family, your extended family, your neighborhood, your social media followers, and ultimately to the world. This kind of work on yourself is the biggest thing you can do to contribute to creating more love, compassion, and peace in the world. Welcome to your path to changing the world one emotion at a time.

This book is a guide to experiencing the deep peace that comes from learning to be completely at home with yourself, exactly as you are in this moment in your life. As you learn to gain power over your emotions, fears and insecurities that have kept you stuck no longer have power over you, and you are able to step into the life of your dreams.

There are ten guided meditations in this book, and each one builds on the previous one.

1. We first learn to be fully present in our body.
2. We become an observer of our emotions.
3. We learn to identify the physical reaction that different emotions create in our body and also learn where we store different emotions in our body.
4. We focus on the "bad" emotions of anger, grief, fear, shame, guilt, and learn to acknowledge, welcome, and honor them as a part of ourselves. We end with the meditation that teaches you to cultivate joy.

5. Experience the peace that comes with becoming a fully integrated human being.
6. We learn how to use these processes to gain power over the multitude of emotions that arise as we step out into the world into our biggest life.

A final note: In each chapter, before I introduce you to the meditation for that emotion, I describe one of my experiences with that emotion. When reading the vignette on the emotions, I may come across as a victim. If you get that impression, it would be correct. We all have an inner victim. The point of the meditations is to move you from a victim position to a position of power. That is the intention for this whole book: to go from being a victim of your circumstances and emotions to becoming an integrated human being who is no longer on a roller coaster between elation and desperation based on whether or not you feel you are acceptable to society at large. The roller-coaster ride stops when you become fully acceptable to yourself. The magic that I hope we will create by doing this work is that as we learn to accept ourselves, flaws and all, we will be able to be more accepting of other human beings in our life, and as more and more of us do this, we end up in a world with less hostility and more compassion.

Preparing for the meditations

As you are learning these skills, it is best if you do these meditations in the same place every day. I often meditate on my bed—so there is no need for a special room. A clutter-free space helps, because it helps your mind be clutter-free as well.

Practicing in the same space has a few benefits

It helps train the mind and body to slip into the "meditative mode" more easily.

The space itself acquires an energy that is peaceful and gentle with repeated practice.

Later on, as you learn to slip into these practices "on the go," bringing up the image of this special space in your mind brings in that energy of peace and quiet and the mental image becomes a safe haven.

I will also say that if the choice is between clearing the clutter and doing the meditation, I would choose the meditation. As you make it a regular practice and your mind becomes clutter-free, your outer environment will follow suit.

I suggest that you do this first thing in the morning or last thing at night.

Let us get started!

1. FULLY EMBODIED

This meditation helps you to practice coming into your body and being fully present and fully embodied.

Practically, what that means is being aware of having a body and being in it. When we are worried, living in the past or worrying about our future, we tend to be present just in and around our heads and we are in auto-pilot mode with respect to our bodies.

Before you start this meditation take a minute to note what your level of anxiety is. Is your mind racing with all the things you must do?

Are you upset with yourself for something you did or did not do? Give yourself this gift—a few minutes that are just about you.

1. Sit comfortably, ideally with your feet touching the floor.
2. Take a deep breath, as if you were pulling air from your feet up; feel your abdomen expand and fill your lungs all the way to the top of your shoulders and let out the breath with a sigh.
3. Do this step two more times.
4. As you let your breath assume its normal rhythm, imagine a warm golden light moving up through your feet.
5. Feel your soles warm up; sense your toes filling up; sense both your feet full of this light. As you focus on your feet, pay attention to any sensations, pain, tingling, etc., in your feet. Check to make sure you have your feet flat on the ground. Practice relaxing into the warmth of this light.

6. Feel the light move up your legs, through your ankles. Become aware of your entire lower leg, shins, sides of your legs, calves—all the way to your knees. Let your lower legs ease and relax into this light.

7. The light is moving up your thighs. Become aware of your upper thighs, inner thighs, genitals, lower thighs where your thighs are touching the seat, where your bottom is placed on the seat; both your legs are now filled with and immersed in this warm golden light. Become really present in and aware of your legs. Also become fully aware of how the chair supports you—a metaphor for how the earth supports you.

8. Feel the light moving up your lower torso: lower back, lower abdomen, up through your solar plexus, up your chest and upper back, all the way to your shoulders.

9. Check to see if you are straining your back or clenching your stomach. Do you have pain anywhere? Relax into this warm golden light. Let go into it completely. Feel yourself fully present in your legs and torso.

10. The light is now moving down your shoulders and filling your arms all the way up to the tips of your fingers. You feel your palms open up. Lay palms upwards on your thighs.

11. The warm light also moves up your neck and fills your head and you become aware of your jaw, your cheeks, your eyes, your forehead, all the way to the top of your head.

12. Scan your body quickly now from the top of your head all the way to the soles of your feet. Feel the light in and around you and relax fully into it.

13. In this space of being fully present in your body, become aware of the deep, deep silence that is at your core. There is a deep quietness that is at our center, a deep peace underneath all the busyness of your mind.

14. When you are fully present in your body, you now get to access that silence. Listen into that silence and feel it

> fill you up with its peace. Stay there for a few minutes in that silence.

15. Take a couple of seconds to be fully present in your body and express appreciation for all that is good with it.
16. When you feel complete, take a few deep breaths and bring yourself back into the room.

This is the practice of being fully embodied. As you practice this, you will be able to slip into that silent peace at your core more and more easily.

An exercise to help

Become aware of the stillness that is below everything around you. You can hear the traffic or the AC buzzing, the kids talking (or screaming), etc., but if you take a few minutes to pay attention, you will notice that there is a stillness beneath everything. It is as if it is the stillness that provides a stage to allow all the noise and chatter outside us (and inside us) to exist. Seek that ground of stillness every time you find yourself spiraling into chaos.

Journal exercises

What was your state of mind before you started the meditation?
Did you reach that still, quiet place at your core?
*(It is OK if you were only there for a fleeting second—as you
keep practicing you will be able to stay there longer.)*
What did you leave behind as you entered that space?
Take a few minutes to describe the sensation
of sitting in that quiet space.

Write your answers to these questions in the blank space below

2. BECOMING AWARE OF THE OBSERVER

In the last meditation, we learned how to be fully present in our body and just sit there for a minute, and how to become aware of the silence underneath and at the core of our being. And we also expressed appreciation for our body, just because our body does so much, and we ignore it so much.

In this meditation, we want to build on what we learned in the last meditation.

We get fully into our body and then learn to slip into the "observer" mode. Think back to the last time you felt an unpleasant emotion such as anger or sadness and paint the picture of the event in your mind.

Look at yourself in that situation.

Do you see how the emotion consumed you?

There was no awareness of your body; there was just the emotion, for example: anger.

You were the anger.

You had no power over the emotion.

This meditation helps us to separate from our emotions and watch our emotions instead of being them. Once we become the observer instead of the emotion, we gain back our power. Then we are able to work with the emotion and do with the emotion what we want to do with it instead of being so immersed in it that we can't separate ourselves from it.

Visualization of an emotion

1. Sit comfortably, with your feet touching the floor.
2. Take a deep breath, as if you were pulling air from your feet up; feel your abdomen expand and fill your lungs all the way to the top of your shoulders and let out the breath with a sigh.
3. Do this step two more times.
4. As with the last meditation, focus on your feet. Imagine a warm golden light filling your feet.
5. Feel the light move up your legs; sense your ankles, calves, shins, your entire lower leg filled with this light.
6. Let the light move up and fill your entire leg—from the soles of your feet all the way to your hips.
7. Sense it now moving up and filling your torso: lower abdomen, lower back, mid-back, mid-abdomen, through your heart space, see it fill your entire body from the soles of your feet to your shoulders and arms.
8. See the light move up now to fill your neck and head. Scan your entire body that is filled with this light from the top of your head to the soles of your feet.
9. As you relax fully into this warm golden light that has filled you, travel for a minute once again to the silence at your core. Listen to that silence and experience the peace within you, always present, just waiting for you to access it.
10. Now anchored in the space of quietness—bring back the image you painted earlier of a recent time when you were really upset, angry, sad, or anxious.
11. Notice what happens to the light within you.
12. Is the light that filled your body missing in some spots?

13. Become fully aware of how this emotion affects you physically.
14. Where in your body does the emotion live?
15. What are the sensations associated with this emotion?
16. Is it pain?
17. Is it numbness?
18. Notice your breath—has it changed?
19. Is it coming in spurts?
20. Are you holding your breath?
21. How does it compare to the steady long breaths you had started the session with?
22. You have become the observer of the emotion. You are not immersed in it.
23. As you observe it, can you see that it will not consume you? It will just rise and fall. You can allow it, its rhythm. You are not it. You are the observer of this phenomenon.

Journal exercise

What emotion did you bring up?
Where does it live in your body?
What were the physical sensations?
How was being the observer different from being the emotion?
Did you feel uncomfortable watching the emotion?
Was there a sense of loss?

Write your answers to these questions in the blank space below

____

____

____

____

____

3. GETTING TO KNOW YOUR OBSERVER

In this meditation, we are focusing on getting to know the observer in you.

The meditation is very similar to the previous one, but the focus is different.

1. Sit comfortably, with your feet touching the floor.
2. Take a deep breath, as if you were pulling air from your feet up; feel your abdomen expand and fill your lungs all the way to the top of your shoulders and let out the breath with a sigh. Do this step two more times.
3. As with the last meditation, focus on your feet. Imagine a warm golden light filling your feet.
4. Feel the light move up your legs; sense your ankles, calves, shins, and your entire lower leg filled with this light.
5. Let the light move up and fill your entire leg—from the soles of your feet all the way to your hips.
6. Sense it now moving up and filling your torso: lower abdomen, lower back, mid back, mid-abdomen, up your heart space. See it fill your entire body from the soles of your feet to your shoulders and arms.
7. See the light move up now to fill your neck and head. Scan your entire body that is filled with this light from the top of your head to the soles of your feet.
8. As you relax fully into this warm golden light that has filled you, travel for a minute once again to the silence at

your core. Listen to that silence and experience the peace within you; it is always present, and just waiting for you to access it. Now anchored in the space of quietness—bring back the image you painted earlier of a recent time when you were really upset, angry, sad, or anxious.

9. Notice what happens to the light within you.

10. Where in your body does the darkness of that emotion reside?

11. As you begin to notice where the emotion is and what it feels like, do you see that you have separated yourself from the emotion. You have become the observer of the emotion.

12. Pay attention to where you are observing from. Are you observing the sensation from the back of your body? Are you above looking down? Are you in the front looking in?

13. Wherever your observer lives, get familiar with how living there feels.

14. Listen into the silence at your core; that silence at your core is messaging that all is well. Feel into the peace that the silence brings.

15. Even as you observe the unpleasant emotion, the observer in you is not feeling the unpleasant emotion.

16. Feel into that peace in your observer persona.

17. Stay there for two minutes—counting silently using your fingers

18. At the end of two minutes, gently bring yourself back into the room.

19. Open your eyes.

20. Keep the awareness of the peace within your observer with you as long as possible.

Journal exercise

Where does your observer live?
Did you get to sense the peace that is inherent to the observer?
This unshakable peace comes from the observer's
knowing that s/he is never affected by these emotions or
by the activity that produced that emotion. Spend some
time in this observer stance and ask the question:
"What would you like to tell me today?"
Write down whatever comes to you without removing
your pen from the page until you feel complete.

Write your answers to these questions in the blank space below

4. WORKING WITH ANGER

From this meditation onwards, we are working with individual emotions and how they manifest within us. In this one, we work with anger.

We learn what this emotion feels like physically through watching the version of us that experienced it.

We learn to be OK with feeling it. We stop pushing it away and instead look at it, feel it fully, and welcome it in as a part of our experience of life in the moment.

Before we get into these meditations, I want to say two things. When I ask you to bring up an incident in which you remember feeling angry—allow your subconscious mind to bring up whatever is ready to be healed. For each of these subsequent meditations, the incident that pops up in your mind is the one that is ready to be healed.

Now, depending on the intensity of the incident, it will likely take more than one session of the meditation to heal it. Be patient with yourself. The version of you in the incident that has felt shunned and judged for many years may not be willing to be welcomed into your heart the minute you invite him/her back. Give her/him time. Every time you repeat the meditation, you will notice a loosening of the resistance.

Vignette: A memory of anger & what it feels like to me

We lived in a two-bedroom apartment in Mumbai. My parents slept in one bedroom, my aunt and uncle in the other, and all the rest of us (I think at the time four people for sure and any guests who stopped by, which was frequently) slept on the living room floor on roll-up futons. To say that it was a crowded space is being generous.

I was about fifteen years old. My oldest brother was twenty. Throughout my life to that point, he was constantly complaining and berating me about my lack of attention to dressing up. To be fair to him, I was a teenager that had no clue about how to dress. I did not care (at least outwardly) about how I looked, and also did not think it made any difference, because no one had ever told me that I was pretty. All I had heard about was about my flat nose and habit of sucking on my tongue; not one single person in those fifteen years had stopped to tell me that I was beautiful. It was not until I got to college and received compliments on my "straight nose" and beautiful eyes and eyelashes did I have a sense that there might be a different narrative about my looks. Therefore, it is not really surprising that I did not pay attention to whether or not my clothes were ironed or what I did to my face, but I digress.

That morning, my brother was upset because I was not wearing a *bindi* or kohl. Never mind that I went to a Catholic school and I could not openly display Hindu symbols (in a majority Hindu nation, mind you), but he was going on about me not caring. In the background, there was also the issue that the guy who brought our ironed closed every day had for some reason not shown up. I did not have an ironed uniform to wear to school, I had no idea how to iron anything, and I was going to be late to school. All of this chaos, and all my brother could think of was to complain about me not wearing a *bindi* and kohl!

Something flipped inside me, and I yelled, "THIS IS MY FACE! I WILL DO WITH IT WHAT I WANT!" Even as I was yelling, my body was quivering, my voice was unsteady, and I could feel uncontrollable rage spilling out. I felt hot.

I also felt terror. I knew at some level that this was not OK. It was not OK to express anger. It was especially not OK for a young girl to express anger. It was even worse for a younger sister to be disdainful and angry at her older brother. Even though my parents were not nearly as traditional as most parents of their generation, I had crossed a bridge. My father, who almost never expressed anger or interfered, said in a very stern voice, "You will iron your uniform."

Although the dispute with my brother was about *bindi* and kohl, the message was loud and clear. I had been put in my place. My father had come down on the side of my brother and against me, whether he meant to or not consciously. It was not safe to express anger. This was not the first time I had received that message.

The first time that I remember being punished for being angry was when I was about ten years old. I was assigned a chore, to stack some books or tidy them up. The ten-year-old me was upset, because I probably wanted to bury my head in a book. I sulked and made my displeasure clear by slamming some books on the floor. That was it—my Mom stood me up and hit me on my back, on my thighs, on my butt. Looking back now, I see that it is fear that she was acting from—at least I think it was—or just frustration caused by others. There was plenty of that to go around in a joint family with its fair share of drama queens. But as I sat on a couch sobbing my heart out, bewildered and terrified, the message early on was that you dare not express anger against authority. Again—it was not intentional in that my mother was not hitting me because she wanted me to know that expressing anger was dangerous. She was frustrated; when I acted out, she hit me.

The purpose of including this incident here is to show you why we learn to suppress strong emotions. We learn early and often that it is much safer to suppress strong emotions. It takes a lot of emotional energy to do this. One of the objectives of this course is to help you to stop doing that and instead to release that energy to create the life that you dream of.

So, what did anger feel like to me? It was a full body experience: the entire body was quivering, the body felt warm. It felt like it was full of uncontrollable, unconstrained energy. It was powerful but terrifying, because it was uncontrollable. It was also terrifying because unleashing it had consequences that were not safe. The color associated with the emotion was red.

When you bring up this memory in the role of an observer, you do not feel the unconstrained, uncontrollable energy. You see a part of you: a long-repressed part of you feeling that anger—even if it is a full body experience. As the observer, you have control. As the observer, you can expand your energy and allow the part of you in that memory that you have suppressed forever to be seen, heard, and acknowledged. As you do this, and you welcome this angry part of you into your heart, you learn to love yourself unconditionally. You learn to see that the part of you that felt that anger is not bad; s/he does not need to be pushed down and controlled. S/he needs to be acknowledged and validated.

This practice of bringing into your open heart all aspects of yourself so you can love yourself fully and honor all your experiences is the ultimate goal of this course.

As you repeat these meditations with different emotions and different experiences in which these emotions arose, you will begin to feel your energy come together more powerfully to create a fully integrated person who is completely at peace in her/his skin.

This next meditation teaches you to do just that.

Pre-meditation journal exercise

When was the first time you remember being really angry?

Have you ever allowed yourself to be angry: to really feel anger or even rage?

Write this sentence down at the top of the page in your journal "It is not safe to feel my anger because ..."

Set the timer for a minimum of ten minutes and write without editing and taking your pen off the page.

This kind of meditative writing allows your mind to access the unconscious and helps you see what you have learned about anger and its impact on you and others.

Where did you feel the anger?

Reflect on whether you have chronic pain in your body and whether or not it may be associated with suppressed anger/rage. When did it start? What were the circumstances in your life then? Even if the pain started as a result of a physical accident, it is possible that it is related to suppressed emotions—typically anger. Understanding how and why can help you reduce the impact of anger on your body.

Write your answers to these questions in the blank space below

Meditation to open your heart to anger

These meditations may all seem identical, but it is very important that you sit down and do each of these with the different emotions. The purpose of the course is to integrate all of you—all of your experiences.

1. Sit comfortably, with your feet touching the floor.
2. Take a deep breath, as if you were pulling air from your feet up; feel your abdomen expand and fill your lungs all the way to the top of your shoulders and let out the breath with a sigh. Do this step two more times.
3. As with the last meditation, focus on your feet. Imagine a warm golden light filling your feet.
4. Feel the light move up your legs; sense your ankles, calves, shins, and your entire lower leg filled with this light.
5. Let the light move up and fill your entire leg—from the soles of your feet all the way to your hips.
6. Sense it now moving up and filling your torso: lower abdomen, lower back, mid-back, mid-abdomen, up your heart space. See it fill your entire body from the soles of your feet to your shoulders and arms.
7. See the light move up now to fill your neck and head. Scan your entire body that is filled with this light from the top of your head to the soles of your feet.
8. As you relax fully into this warm golden light that has filled you, travel for a minute once again to the silence at your core. Listen to that silence and experience the peace within you. It is always present, just waiting for you to access it.
9. Remember where your observer lives.
10. Slip into the space and stance of the observer.
11. Now anchored in the space of quietness—let your mind take you to an incident in which you felt the anger.
12. Observe the incident from your observer. You are not re-experiencing the anger.

13. You are observing the part of you that is still carrying the memory of that anger.

14. The observer in you is holding space for that part of you. Take a breath and look at you in that incident as if you were watching a movie.

15. Remember that you are in a safe space. It is safe for you to be angry here.

16. As this scene plays out on the movie screen of your mind,

17. Where in your body does that anger live? We often push the energy of the anger down into our muscles where it becomes muscle memory and may cause pain or other physical discomfort.

18. What does it feel like?

19. Look at the image of the part of you that is feeling that anger.

20. How old is s/he?

21. Is there fear, or maybe terror, at feeling this anger?

22. Look at him or her. How old is she? How is she standing/sitting in that space? Look at her face, palms, and feet.

23. As the observer, I want you to be aware that you're looking at this person not with judgment but with a complete unconditional, non-judgmental presence.

24. Allow that persona, that part of you, to be exactly who he or she is in this moment. There is nothing wrong, it's just what it is, and what it is, is perfect.

25. Be in that space as the observer just looking, acknowledging, witnessing. Then, take a deep breath and as you breathe out, see and feel a beam of golden light moving from your heart towards this part of you in the movie scene.

26. Become aware of the physical sensations this little person is feeling.

27. Hug her/him with your energy. In your mind, say to her, "You are safe. I am here, holding you. Breathe into what you are feeling. It is OK. You are held. I am here. You can relax."

28. As you let this emotion and the part of you that feels it exist, see the light envelop him/her.

29. The observer in you and the light returning to embrace the emotion are signaling that it is safe for this part of you to exist. It does not have to be suppressed anymore.

30. What you are signaling is that it is possible to feel this anger safely without hurting you or anyone else.

31. Allow the anger in and acknowledge it. Acknowledge that it was a warranted emotion given the circumstances and allow it to rise and fall as you and this part of you, breathing together, send the signal that feeling the anger will not destroy you.

32. Feel your heart opening and see the little angry and fearful you relaxing and moving closer into your heart space.

33. As s/he steps in, feel the release, see the shoulders relax, see the little head move up and look the observer in their eyes.

34. S/he is no longer afraid, no longer disallowed or suppressed. S/he is fully integrated in your life.

35. Spend some time here in this space of acceptance allowing yourself to feel the love flowing into your heart.

36. Say "I LOVE ME!" a few times before you come out of the meditation.

Post-meditation journal exercises

What gave rise to the anger?
Do you see that it was something unjust?
What has it shown you about how you could have
acted differently (whether it was laying down clear
boundaries or listening more carefully)?
What is the gift of the experience?

Write your answers in the space below

5. WORKING WITH SADNESS

Deep sadness, like anger, is another emotion we feel frightened of giving into completely. We are afraid that if we let ourselves fully feel the sadness we may never recover and live normally again. However, pushing deep sadness down and refusing to feel it fully is like pushing a part of our experience away and refusing to experience a part of our lives. What ends up happening is that we close off parts of ourselves; this is what people who talk about shamanic journeys are probably referring to when they say that you leave parts of your soul in the past. Portions of you are not accessible, and that means that you do not have access to your full self.

In this next meditation, we will focus on an incident that broke your heart.

For most of us who have lived to adulthood, there are probably several instances when we felt our heart break. As you decide on which heartbreaking incident in your life to work with, my suggestion is to go to the earliest incident that you can remember. Beginning with that first memory of heartbreak and learning to welcome it fully into your experience is a great way to set up a foundation to incorporate all subsequent instances a little bit more easily into your heart. Do not spend too much time trying to identify the incident, though; as I said earlier, the incident that is ready to be healed and welcomed will be the one that first shows up.

Vignette of a broken heart

It was a dark night in Bombay (this was before the city's name changed). Curled up in a corner of the balcony of our two-bedroom apartment was the eight-year-old me. My body was racked with sobs. I had just been pushed out of the group of friends that I had been a part of for nearly three years. A new family with two daughters had moved in. The group had changed. The new family who had moved in spoke the same language as my best friend and I was suddenly the outsider. I was ridiculed and teased. I was shamed and finally unceremoniously and very cruelly pushed out of the group. I felt empty at my core as if I was not a person anymore; it hurt. It was as if the insides of my little body had been gouged out. I felt completely abandoned. I had no idea why someone with whom I had played together for nearly three years suddenly hated me as much as she seemed to now. I was not old enough to formulate clear questions about the whys and wherefores. I assumed that it was something about me. I had been rejected, so it must have been because of me.

As I travel back and look at that little body, I am amazed that such a tiny body, having lived such a short life, can feel the depth of grief I felt. It is as if she is reaching into a reservoir of sadness, bewilderment, and fear that has no bottom. I remember also understanding that my mom did not know how to help me. She did not have the instinct to just hold me and allow the grief but make me feel safe. This was entirely out of her experience. She could neither understand the politics of "mean girls" nor the depth of grief I was experiencing. The only way she knew to comfort me was by making fun of it. This added to the sense of pain and emptiness I felt inside. There was pain, an aching and emptiness. It was dark inside. The instinct was to curl up and protect my insides. The sense of abandonment meant that I could not trust anyone to help. The lessons I learned were that I was alone in the world and that it was not safe to ever be that vulnerable again. The accompanying vow that I made to myself was that I would not ever open my heart to the same degree again and be that defenseless.

We all learn these lessons early. My response to these experiences which taught me not to be vulnerable was to stop expecting help and therefore to stop asking for help. Doing the meditation to heal this experience will begin the process of opening your heart and inviting help in again. This is important because we live in an interdependent world. The ability to ask for and receive help is also intimately connected to the ability to receive everything good. There are risks, but it is true that we have to take risks to experience great rewards.

Pre-meditation journal exercise

Think of an incident that you associate with deep sadness or grief.

Write this sentence down at the top of the page in your journal: "I cannot allow myself to feel this sadness because if I did …." Set the timer for a minimum of ten minutes and write without editing and taking your pen off the page.

This kind of meditative writing allows your mind to access the unconscious and helps you see what you have learned about allowing yourself to feel sad and its impact on you and others.

Where in your body do you feel the sadness or grief?

What does it feel like?

Write your answers to these questions in the blank space below

____

____

____

____

Meditation to heal deep grief and open your heart

These meditations may all seem identical, but it is very important that you sit down and do each of these with the different emotions. The purpose of the course is to integrate all of you—all of your experiences.

1. Sit comfortably, with your feet touching the floor.
2. Take a deep breath, feeling the breath fill you up from your abdomen all the way to your shoulder blades and let the breath out with a sigh. Do this step two more times.
3. As with the last meditation, focus on your feet. Imagine a warm golden light filling your feet.
4. Feel the light move up your legs. Sense your ankles, calves, shins, and your entire lower leg filled with this light.
5. Let the light move up and fill your entire leg, from the soles of your feet all the way to your hips.
6. Sense it now moving up and filling your torso: lower abdomen, lower back, mid-back, mid-abdomen, up your heart space. See it fill your entire body from the soles of your feet to your shoulders and arms.
7. See the light move up now to fill your neck and head. Scan your entire body that is filled with this light from the top of your head to the soles of your feet.
8. As you relax fully into this warm golden light that has filled you, travel for a minute once again to the silence at your core. Listen to that silence and experience the peace within you. It is always present, just waiting for you to access it.
9. Now anchored in the space of quietness, let your mind take you to an incident in which you felt that deep sadness. As I said before, the incident that is ready to be healed will show up.
10. As this scene plays out in the movie screen of your mind, become aware of the warmth and light within you.

11. Notice what happens to the light within you. Where in your body does the darkness of that sadness reside?

12. It is as if there were a space where there is no light, where all the divinity suddenly had to move out to make space for this part of you that is refusing to let the divinity in.

13. In this darkness, can you see the part of you that is sad? Can you see as I saw, that image of you who is feeling that grief?

14. As you observe this space, breath deeply; become aware of the persona within you that is experiencing the sadness. It may just be a silhouette, or it might be a fully fleshed-out part of you.

15. Look at him or her. How old is she? How is she standing or sitting in that space? Look at her face, palms, and feet.

16. As the observer, I want you to be aware that you're looking at this person not with judgment but with a complete unconditional, non-judgmental presence.

17. Allow that persona, that part of you, to be exactly who he or she is in this moment. There is nothing wrong; it's just what it is, and what it is, is perfect.

18. Be in that space as the observer just looking, acknowledging, witnessing. Then, take a deep breath and as you breathe out feel and see a warm golden ray of light and love traveling from your heart to the part of you that is feeling the grief.

19. Become aware of the physical sensations this little person is feeling. Let her/him feel all the pain and emptiness in her/his body.

20. As you let this emotion and the part of you that feels it exist, see the light return envelope him/her.

21. The observer in you and the light returning to embrace the emotion are signaling that it is safe for this part of you to exist.

22. As the observer, What you are signaling is that it is possible to fully feel this emotion fully, and that allowing the grief in and feeling it in your body will not destroy you.

23. Feel your heart opening and see the observer in you welcome the deeply sad you into your heart space.
24. As s/he steps in, feel the release, see the shoulders relax, see the little head move up and look the observer in the eyes.
25. S/he is no longer afraid, no longer disallowed or suppressed. S/he is fully integrated in your life.

Post-meditation journal exercises

What gave rise to the sadness?
Do you see that feeling it fully did not destroy you?
What has it shown you about how you
might react to grief in the future?
Is there another event that you can allow in
right now and fully feel the grief of?
What is the gift of the experience?
Write your answers to these questions in the space below.

Write your answers to these questions in the blank space below.

____

6. WORKING WITH TERROR

All of my primary and secondary schooling was in schools that were run by the Catholic church. Almost all them were named after Catholic saints. The school I attended from kindergarten through eighth grade was St. Anne's, and ninth through eleventh was St. Xavier's. The catchment area for these schools included neighborhoods that were slum colonies. It is a testament to the education policy in India that these children did get a chance to come to school and potentially improve their lives. Attending school, however, did not protect them from the implications of living in a neighborhood that was often ravaged by violence. We had a system of school monitors. This was a student in the class who "monitored" the class when the teacher stepped out. I have no idea why the teacher stepped out or why the class monitor had power. He or she would write the names of children who misbehaved (primarily talked when they were not supposed to) on the board; he or she unbelievably could also use a twelve-inch wooden ruler to discipline (read: hit) his/her classmates. This just blows me away when I think about it. How or why were we given such power? It seems so ridiculous and barbaric now. Not to mention that if any one teacher or class monitor had touched my child, I would have raised hell in that school. In any case, that was the system, and I was almost always picked to be the class monitor in most of my primary classes.

In third grade, two sisters from a slum colony in Mahim were in my class. The older, stronger one was tough and wore an "I don't care" attitude as her armor; the younger, smaller, weaker child was soft and vulnerable and cried easily. Although the details are fuzzy in my mind, I believe that during one of these periods of class monitoring, I disciplined (read: hit) one of these sisters. The younger one became hysterical. As she sobbed and screamed and tried to talk through her grief, I gathered that there had been a gang fight in her neighborhood and her uncle's leg had been cut off. It was not surprising that seeing me hit her sister had allowed the dam of fear to burst. I feel so ashamed of my role in this. The realization that the circumstances in which my classmates existed were starkly different from the comparatively protected and secure life I lived was heartbreaking.

That night was the first of many in which I had a recurring nightmare that unfolded thusly.

The younger sister of the duo had come home to play with me. She had a black string around her neck and a small teddy bear-like figure hung from it. Somehow, we ended up in the hallway of my apartment. Close to the ceiling were clotheslines that had been cleared of all the clothes. It was just her and me in the apartment, and suddenly there was this huge person: big and dark and terrifying. She wanted us to do something. I do not recall what. All I recall is the terror. There was no escape. We were locked in place by her size. I wanted to scream but no sound would come out of my mouth. My body was quivering. I was frozen in place, and suddenly I was alone with this monster and the little teddy bear that was around my friend's neck was hanging from the clothesline. The nightmare ended here but the terror I felt lasted for years. Similar to anger, terror for me was a full-body experience. My throat felt dry and stuck. The body felt like it wanted to shrink and hide away, curl up, and disappear. The colors associated are various shades of gray. When you do the journal exercises below focus on the incident but also on what it felt like in the body. Are there colors you associate with the incident, or sounds and smells? The more clearly you see the incident, the deeper the healing.

Pre-Meditation Exercise Journal exercise

Think of an incident that you associate with terror.

Write this sentence down at the top of the page in your journal: "I cannot allow myself to feel this because if I did …." Set the timer for a minimum of ten minutes and write without editing and taking your pen off the page.

This kind of meditative writing allows your mind to access the unconscious and helps you see what you have learned about allowing yourself to feel terror and its impact on you and others.

Where in your body do you feel the terror?

What does it feel like?

Write your answers to these questions in the blank space below

____

____

____

____

____

____

____

____

____

____

Meditation to make terror a friend

These meditations may all seem identical, but it is very important that you sit down and do each of these with the different emotions. The purpose of the course is to integrate all of you—all of your experiences.

1. Sit comfortably, with your feet touching the floor.
2. Take a deep breath, feeling the breath fill you up from your abdomen all the way to your shoulder blades and let out the breath with a sigh. Do this step two more times.
3. As with the last meditation, focus on your feet. Imagine a warm golden light filling your feet.
4. Feel the light move up your legs. Sense your ankles, calves, shins, and your entire lower leg filled with this light.
5. Let the light move up and fill your entire leg—soles of your feet all the way to your hips.
6. Sense it now moving up and filling your torso: lower abdomen, lower back, mid-back, mid-abdomen, up your heart space. See it fill your entire body from soles of your feet to your shoulders and arms.
7. See the light move up now to fill your neck and head. Scan your entire body that is filled with this light from the top of your head to the soles of your feet.
8. As you relax fully into this warm golden light that has filled you, travel for a minute once again to the silence at your core. Listen to that silence and experience the peace within you. It is always present, just waiting for you to access it.
9. Remember where your observer lives.
10. Slip into the space and stance of the observer.

11. Now anchored in the space of quietness, let your mind take you to an incident in which you felt that terror.

12. Observe the incident from your observer. You are not re-experiencing the terror.

13. You are observing the part of you that is still carrying the memory of that terror.

14. The observer in you is holding space for that part of you. Take a breath and look at yourself in that incident as if you were watching a movie.

15. Remember that you are in a safe space.

16. As this scene plays out on the movie screen of your mind, become aware of the warmth and light within you.

17. Notice what happens to the light within you. Where in your body does that terror live?

18. What does it feel like?

19. Look at the image of the part of you that is feeling that terror.

20. How old is s/he?

21. See yourself welcoming her/him into your space.

22. Look at him or her. How old is s/he? How is s/he standing or sitting in that space? Look at her face, palms, and feet.

23. As the observer, I want you to be aware that you're looking at this person not with judgment but with a complete unconditional, non-judgmental presence.

24. Allow that persona, that part of you, to be exactly who he or she is in this moment. There is nothing wrong; it's just what is and what it is, is perfect.

25. Be in that space as the observer just looking, acknowledging, witnessing. Then, take a deep breath and let it go.

26. Become aware of the physical sensations this little person is feeling.

27. Hug her/him with your energy. In your mind, say to her/him, "You are safe. I am here, holding you. Breathe into what you are feeling. It is OK. You are held. I am here. You can relax."

28. As you let this emotion and the part of you that feels it exist, see the light return. Let the light that was pushed aside to make way for the darkness of this emotion shine its light on it.

29. The observer in you and the light returning to embrace the emotion are signaling that it is safe for this part of you to exist. It does not have to be suppressed anymore.

30. What you are signaling is that it is possible to fully feel this emotion. Allowing the terror in, acknowledging it, and allowing it to rise and fall as you and this part of you breathes together, is sending the signal that feeling this emotion will not destroy you.

31. Feel your heart opening and see the little terrified you relaxing and moving closer into your heart space.

32. As s/he steps in, feel the release, see the shoulders relax, see the little head move up and look the observer in the eyes.

33. S/he is no longer afraid, no longer disallowed or suppressed. S/he is fully integrated in your life.

Post-meditation journal exercises

What gave rise to the terror?
Do you see that feeling it fully did not destroy you?
What has it shown you about how you
might react to fear in the future?
Is there another fearful event that you can
allow in right now and fully feel?
What is the gift of the experience?

Write your answers to these questions in the blank space below

7. JEALOUSY

In the United States today (May 2020), we have the clearest example of jealousy caused by a deep, deep sense of insecurity. It is manifestly evident in the way President Trump talks about and treats his predecessor President Obama. It is so clear that he feels exceptionally insecure because of all the adoration that Obama engenders. I can almost see the little boy inside him who needs so much to be the center of attention and is terrified of becoming irrelevant.

I know the feeling well because I have felt it throughout my life. My clearest memory of the first time I felt it was when my aunt delivered a baby girl.

As the sole girl child in an extended Nair family that still practiced some aspects of a matrilineal society, being the only child in my generation that would carry the family name forward was the only thing that made me special. I was already competing with my older brothers for attention and had received plenty of messages about not being quite as smart as them, as special as them, or as important as them. The only thing I had going for me in my eight- or nine-year-old mind was this special privilege of being the only girl child in the extended family, and now with the birth of this baby, that was gone as well. What was worse was that she was gorgeous and seemed to have every physical feature that I lacked: a fairer skin, a beautiful rosebud like nose, big beautiful large eyes, etc.

By the age of eight or ten, I had constantly been told about my ugly flat nose, was mercilessly teased about it, and even had wooden clothes-pegs on my nose to make it sharper. I do not remember one instance when I was told that I was beautiful, which was a tragedy because I was a stunningly beautiful young child and woman but I never felt the power that a woman gains from knowing that. The conversation around my little cousin, on the other hand, was constantly about how beautiful she was, how perfect her little nose was and how flawless her lips were, etc. Every time I heard family members talk about her, I felt like a little part inside me died—my chest hurt and my heart broke. This sense of hurt and growing inadequacy was difficult to hide. Adults around me who noticed it then spent time teasing me about being jealous. So not only did I feel jealous, but I also felt terrible for feeling jealous. The feeling of jealousy is a combination of grief for oneself and anger towards the person you are jealous of. It is one of those emotions that you hate feeling and shame yourself most for feeling.

One of the goals of the vignettes in this book is to demonstrate that all these emotions are universal and always spontaneous reactions to circumstances. So, feeling shame for feeling them and pushing them away and/or refusing to acknowledge these is asking the impossible. It also takes an enormous amount of energy to suppress these aspects of ourselves. It puts an impossible burden on us. We are not meant to be perfect. The "negative" emotions are what add spice to our experience of life. We become complete and fully rounded human beings when we stop pushing them away and welcome them as an honored part of our experience of life.

Journal exercises

How do you react when I suggest that you may be jealous?
Are you resistant to the idea that you may be jealous?
How does your body react?
Stay with these sensations for some time to really understand
your reaction to the word and everything it conveys to you.
Write this sentence down at the top of the page in your
journal "People who feel jealous are terrible because …."

Set the timer for a minimum of ten minutes and write
without editing and taking your pen off the page.
This kind of meditative writing allows your mind to access the
unconscious and helps you see what you have learned about
allowing yourself to feel jealous and its impact on you and others.
Pay attention to all the other emotions that are associated with
the jealousy—insecurity born out of a sense of inadequacy,
heartache, sense of abandonment, rejection, anger, shame.
This is a complex experience, so be sure to
recognize each component part of it.

Now after those exercises are you able to admit that you have felt
jealous? When did you first feel jealous?

**Write your answers to these
questions in the blank space below**

Meditation to be A-OK with jealousy

These meditations may all seem identical, but it is very important that you sit down and do each of these with the different emotions. The purpose of the course is to integrate all of you—all of your experiences.

1. Sit comfortably, with your feet touching the floor.
2. Take a deep breath, feeling the breath fill you up from your lower abdomen all the way to your shoulder blades, and let the breath out with a sigh. Do this step two more times.
3. As with the last meditation, focus on your feet. Imagine a warm golden light filling your feet.
4. Feel the light move up your legs. Sense your ankles, calves, shins, and your entire lower leg filled with this light.
5. Let the light move up and fill your entire leg—from the soles of your feet all the way to your hips.
6. Sense it now moving up and filling your torso: lower abdomen, lower back, mid-back, mid-abdomen, up your heart space. See it fill your entire body from the soles of your feet to your shoulders and arms.
7. See the light move up now to fill your neck and head. Scan your entire body that is filled with this light from the top of your head to the soles of your feet.
8. As you relax fully into this warm golden light that has filled you, travel for a minute once again to the silence at your core. Listen to that silence and experience the peace within you, always present, just waiting for you to access it.
9. Remember where your observer lives.
10. Slip into the space and stance of the observer.
11. Now anchored in the space of quietness—let your mind take you to an incident in which you felt jealous.
12. Observe the incident from your observer. You are not jealous now.
13. You are observing the part of you that is still carrying the memory of being jealous.

14. The observer in you is holding space for that part of you. Take a breath and look at yourself in that incident as if you were watching a movie.
15. Remember that you are in a safe space.
16. As this scene plays out on the movie screen of your mind, bring in the person you are jealous of as well.
17. As the observer who is not affected by the jealousy and is holding space for the part of you that felt insecure, slighted, inadequate, etc., the observer is able to bring in both the part of you that is jealous and the person(s) you are jealous of.
18. Where in your body does that jealousy live? Where does the shame you feel about feeling jealous live? Where does the pain of heartbreak you feel at the comparison live? Where does the anger you feel towards that person live?
19. Look at the image of the part(s) of you that is/are feeling this mixture of emotions.
20. How old is s/he?
21. Look at him or her.
22. How is she standing or sitting in that space? Look at her face, palms, and feet.
23. As the observer, I want you to be aware that you're looking at this person(s) not with judgment but with a complete unconditional, non-judgmental presence.
24. Allow that persona, that part of you, to be exactly who he or she is in this moment. There is nothing wrong; it's just what it is, and what it is, is perfect.
25. Be in that space as the observer just looking, acknowledging, and witnessing. Then, take a deep breath and let it go.
26. Become aware of the physical sensations this little person is feeling.
27. Hug her/him with your energy. In your mind say to her, "You are safe. I am here, holding you. Breathe into what you are feeling. It is OK. You are held. I am here. You can relax."

28. As you let this emotion and the part of you that feels it exist, see the light return. Let the light that was pushed aside to make way for the darkness of this jealousy and the shame associated with it shine its light on it.

29. The observer in you and the light returning to embrace the jealousy, shame, and anger are signaling that it is safe for this part of you to exist. It does not have to be suppressed anymore.

30. What you are signaling is that it is possible to honor this experience and empathize with the you that felt all this. Allowing the terror in, acknowledging it, and allowing it to rise and fall as you and this part of you breathe together is sending the signal that openly acknowledging jealousy and all the attendant emotions does not make you a "bad" person. Honoring and accepting it as part of your experience makes you fully human.

31. Feel your heart opening, and see and feel that insecure jealous part of you relaxing and moving closer into your heart space.

32. As s/he steps in, feel the release, see the shoulders relax, see the little head move up and look the observer in the eyes.

33. S/he is no longer afraid, no longer disallowed or suppressed. S/he is fully integrated in your life.

Write your answers to these questions in the blank space below

____

____

____

____

____

____

____

____

____

8.GUILT/SHAME

The first incident that comes to mind when I think of guilt and shame is that of me cheating in a test. I must have been about seven. I was not prepared for the exam. I think it was a test on Hindi. I was afraid because I sensed I would not do well on the test. I was anticipating the consequences of that in a family that prized academic achievement. At seven I am not sure if I knew how to prepare for a test but I certainly felt guilty because I was not prepared—the shame of not being good enough.

I also felt desperate because I did not want to go home with a bad score and so I peeped at my friend's paper for inspiration. As luck would have it the teacher looked over my way just as I got up the courage to cheat; she yelled at me, gave me a zero on the test and wrote me up. Shame, guilt and fear all rolled up into a huge ball of emotion that a tiny seven-year-old body did not have the skill to defuse. The only release that I had was to burst into tears.

When I think back to that incident, I feel like curling up and disappearing. Every part of my body is cringing. I do not want to be seen. I do not want to be exposed. As much as I want to disappear, I am forced to be on display. I am shamed and ridiculed every time a new member of the extended family hears about the event because in an Indian joint family, there are no boundaries; every individual triumph is celebrated, and every failure advertised and shamed. So every time that story was shared was another moment to desperately want to disappear but be forced into the glare of unrelenting scrutiny and shaming. It left me feeling very unsafe. There was no safe harbor from the guilt and shame.

This might seem like a silly incident to focus on. The meditation that follows will focus on giving that child in that memory her sense of safety back. That memory is quite fresh somewhere in my consciousness and every time I feel unsafe, I react as a seven-year-old rather than the sixty-one-year-old I am. Reaching out to that seven-year-old and holding her in safety helped me to gain back power and stand up to bullies.

Meditation to be A-OK with guilt/shame

These meditations may all seem identical, but it is very important that you sit down and do each of these with the different emotions. The purpose of the course is to integrate all you—all your experiences.

1. Sit comfortably, with your feet touching the floor.
2. Take a deep breath, feeling the breath fill you up from your lower abdomen, all the way to the top of your shoulders and let the breath out with a sigh. Do this step two more times.
3. As with the last meditation, focus on your feet. Imagine a warm golden light filling your feet.
4. Feel the light move up your legs. Sense your ankles, calves, shins, and your entire lower leg filled with this light.
5. Let the light move up and fill your entire leg—from the soles of your feet all the way to your hips.
6. Sense it now moving up and filling your torso: lower abdomen, lower back, mid-back, mid-abdomen, up your heart space. See it fill your entire body from the soles of your feet to your shoulders and arms.
7. See the light move up now to fill your neck and head. Scan your entire body that is filled with this light from the top of your head to the soles of your feet.

8. As you relax fully into this warm golden light that has filled you, travel for a minute once again to the silence at your core. Listen to that silence and experience the peace within you, always present, just waiting for you to access it.
9. Remember where your observer lives.
10. Slip into the space and stance of the observer.
11. Now anchored in the space of quietness—let your mind take you to an incident in which you felt joy.
12. Observe the incident from your observer. You are not feeling guilt or shame now.
13. You are observing the part of you that is still carrying the memory of feeling guilty and ashamed.
14. The observer in you is holding space for that part of you. Take a breath and look at yourself in that incident as if you were watching a movie. The incident is playing on the screen.
15. Remember that you are in a safe space.
16. As the observer who is not affected by the guilt or shame, watch the part of you that felt guilty and ashamed.
17. Where in your body does that guilt/shame live?
18. Look at the image of the image of you that is feeling this mixture of emotions.
19. How old is s/he?
20. Look at him or her.
21. How is she standing or sitting in that space? Look at her face, palms, and feet.
22. As the observer, I want you to be aware that you're looking at this person(s) not with judgment but with a complete unconditional, non-judgmental presence.
23. Allow that persona, that part of you, to be exactly who he or she is in this moment. There is nothing wrong; it's just what it is, and what it is, is perfect.
24. Be in that space as the observer just looking, acknowledging, and witnessing. Take a deep breath. As you breathe out, see and feel a warm golden loving ray of love and light go from your heart to this version of you

that is feeling guilty and ashamed. See this love filled light envelope her/him.

25. Become aware of the physical sensations this person is feeling.

26. Hug her/him with loving energy. In your mind—say to her, "You are safe. I am here, holding you. Breathe into what you are feeling. What you are feeling is legitimate. It is allowed. It is natural. It is OK. You are held. I am here. You can relax."

27. As you let this emotion and the part of you that feels it exist, see the light return. Let the light that was pushed aside to make way for the darkness of this guilt, and the shame associated with it, shine its light on it.

28. The observer in you and the light returning to embrace the guilt and shame are signaling that it is safe for this part of you to exist. It does not have to be suppressed anymore.

29. What you are signaling is that it is possible to honor this experience and empathize with the you that felt all this. Acknowledging the guilt, and allowing it to rise and fall as you and this part of you breathes together, is sending the signal that openly acknowledging guilt and all the attendant emotions does not make you a "bad" person. Honoring and accepting it as part of your experience makes you fully human.

30. Feel your heart opening and see and feel that part of that feels guilty and that has helped keep you feeling not good enough. Understand that s/he can let go now. Feel her/him relaxing and moving closer into your heart space.

31. As s/he steps in, feel the release, see the shoulders relax, see the little head move up and look at you the observer in the eyes.

32. S/he is no longer afraid, no longer disallowed or suppressed. S/he is fully integrated in your life.

9. FEAR OF STEPPING UP

The terror described above is one manifestation of fear—the extreme expression. In that nightmare, I was really terrified for my life. There is, however, a far more common kind of fear that is present in our lives: fear of taking action. This is particularly true when we try to step up and out of our comfort zone in pursuit of a dream.

It came completely out of the blue. I was promoted to a position that, in truth, I had not ever envisioned as part of my career path. I had big dreams, but they were not very well articulated. I knew I had the makings of a leader within me. I had just finished a very successful stint as the president of a community organization. That was also not something I had aspired to. However, as I stood on a stage in front of big crowds as a community leader, I felt completely at home. I felt like I had arrived. I was full of ideas; I felt like I mattered. It was as if this experience in some energetic way had propelled me into the leadership position at work.

So there I was, the unexpected leader of a group of scientists and researchers. I was completely aware of the fact that although I had the ability, I did not have the experience. In fact, I had said as much to the higher-ups that appointed me. It was an appointment for political reasons, and the upshot of that was those who appointed me were expecting me to be a figurehead, but I was never cut out to be one.

What followed were almost three years that were brutal: busy and exhilarating but also painful, humiliating, and debilitating. I experienced abandonment, back-biting, and betrayal of the worst kind. I got caught up in academic politics that I was ill-prepared for. I felt more alone than I had ever felt in my life.

There were consequences beyond my job. The pace of the work and my surprising elevation to a place of prominence created rifts in my marriage. Given the new pace, I could not keep up with all the tasks at home that I used to handle with ease. Something had to give. There were a multitude of other stresses, including minor irritants that blew up into full-blown rifts when all the above was added to the mix. Add to that the stress of my father's falling ill and passing and all the heartache that entailed, and a realization that I had never sat down and figured out what I wanted in life. My life was primed for classic breakdown.

This had been at least thirty years in the making. Even when I was a young eight- or ten-year-old, I knew that I wanted to do something big, that I wanted to be written about and interviewed. There was a knowing deep down that I was meant to experience all that. But then life interfered. My mother died in a plane crash when I was nineteen. I suddenly became responsible for a household with two older brothers—one who was struggling with the throes of early marriage and another who was rapidly descending into alcoholism.

I tried to escape that responsibility by agreeing to an arranged marriage. I became a mom ten months after I got married and ended up right back in Bombay with my birth family while my husband tried to relocate to the Middle East. Once he relocated, we moved over twenty-five times across three continents while raising two kids.

Nearly thirty years later, the stress at the high-powered job, the impact it had on my marriage, and my father's death all resulted in me deciding I needed time off from my responsibilities to the marriage. It felt like I had not taken a full breath since the night my mother's plane crashed and turned my world upside down. It is an overused phrase, I know, but I really needed to find myself.

That search took me a good two-and-a-half years. I believe I did find myself and am becoming better and better at articulating for myself what it is that I want and at asking for it without fear or the emotional manipulation that fear of openly asking for my needs often resulted in.

That experience is relevant to this vignette on fear. I realize that, as I have tried in multiple ways after that to step up into a bigger game and level up, there is a part of me that is terrified—terrified of going through similar trauma and inflicting pain on loved ones again. The terror is a little different. In the first experience it was physical danger that caused the terror resulting in a legitimate fight/flight/freeze response in the body. In this case, the pain I am afraid of is emotional pain. The problem is that for the reptilian part of our brain, both fears are identical and set off the same cascade of fight/flight/freeze responses. This results in our creative brain shutting off. The body is preparing for fight or flight and acting as if we are in physical danger. Survival is paramount; creative solutions and logic are not. If we have experienced this kind of trauma after achieving a big goal, it is almost impossible to work steadily towards another big goal without the fear of repeating your experience sabotaging you in some way. It is very wily, this terror of repeating past trauma. She manifests as procrastination, as inadequate preparation for a presentation or interview, and as perfectionism. To isolate it and capture it to heal it takes an openness and practices that allow you to become the observer of the fear and talk to it. The type of meditation we have practiced so far will help you get to this space.

Journal exercises

If you could wave a magic wand and change something in the life you are living today, what would it be? As human beings, most of us will have multiple aspects of our life we would like to change. Make a list of all these. These are your life goals—right? I would also call these goals dreams. It does not matter if they are "small dreams," e.g., cooking more meals at home or "big dreams" about changing the world by running for public office or anything else. This list gives you a sense of what changes in your life will make you happier.

Take several deep breaths, focus on the list of goals, and identify the things on the list that you feel you have some control over. A common issue might be a healthier body, for example.

Pick one that you have been meaning to act on. A good indicator of which one to focus on is the one that keeps you awake at night— something that you love to hate yourself for.

Write this sentence on the top of your journal page—"I have not taken any (enough) action towards this goal, because I am afraid that if I take a step towards it ..."

Set the timer for a minimum of ten minutes and write without taking your hand off the page.

As I mention in the meditation below some of the most common fears are the following:

How will it affect my role in the family?
What will my parents think?
Can I really do this?
What if I alienate my friends?
I am not sure I have the skills.
Look at what happened the last time I
tried something. It was a failure.

I dare not.
It is safer to stay where I am.
At least I know how to handle these frustrations.
I am not sure what I would have to handle if
I did what I really would love to do.
It is too risky.
If these do not come up when you write and you have
different fears that come up, add those to this list and
examine the list again and see if they resonate.

Write your answers to these questions in the space below

____
____
____
____
____
____
____
____
____
____
____
____
____
____
____
____
____
____
____

Meditation to oercome fear of taking action

For this meditation, we are working with an experience you may have had that is similar to the one I described above—an experience in which you showed up in a big way, in school, at home at work, at church, or in your community, and got hurt. If there isn't an immediate link to an incident, then think of some action that you have been putting off. Sit down with your journal, set your timer for 15 minutes and write the sentence, "I have been putting "X (whatever the action is) off because if I complete it I may have to …." Write without editing or taking your pen off the paper for the full 15 minutes. Your mind will let you know exactly what fear is holding you back. With that in hand, start this meditation which starts off like all the others with getting into your body and slipping into the observer stance. This is also an emotion and experience where an emotional freedom technique (commonly called "tapping") can work wonders. For more about tapping please visit my website: www.seeta2durga.com.

1. Sit comfortably, with your feet touching the floor.
2. Take a deep breath, feeling the breath fill you up from your abdomen all the way to your shoulder blades, and let the breath out with a sigh. Do this step two more times.
3. As with the last meditation, focus on your feet. Imagine a warm golden light filling your feet.
4. Feel the light move up your legs. Sense your ankles, calves, shins, and your entire lower leg filled with this light.
5. Let the light move up and fill your entire leg—from the soles of your feet all the way to your hips.
6. Sense it now moving up and filling your torso: lower abdomen, lower back, mid-back, mid-abdomen, up your heart space. See it fill your entire body from the soles of your feet to your shoulders and arms.

7. See the light move up now to fill your neck and head. Scan your entire body that is filled with this light from the top of your head to the soles of your feet.

8. As you relax fully into this warm golden light that has filled you, travel for a minute once again to the silence at your core. Listen to that silence and experience the peace within you, always present, just waiting for you to access it.

9. Remember where your observer lives.

10. Slip into the space and stance of the observer.

11. Now anchored in the space of quietness—let your mind take you to images of stepping out of your comfort zone to pursue a long-held dream. If you did not have a specific incident come to your mind, take your mind to the fears you wrote about.

12. Observe the thoughts and fears that come up.

13. Observe where they affect you physically or where in your body you "stuff" these fears.

14. Try and personify the fear. What does it look like? Is it a person? Does it look like you or a parent or sibling?

15. Breathe into the part of the body where this fear resides and let it talk to you.

16. You are still in the observer stance. Be in that space as the observer just looking, acknowledging, witnessing. Then, take a deep breath and let it go.

17. Become aware of the physical sensations this little person is feeling.

18. Hug her/him with your energy. In your mind, say to her, "You are safe. I am here, holding you. Breathe into what you are feeling. It is OK. You are held. I am here. You can relax."

19. Feel your heart opening and see the little terrified you relaxing and moving closer into your heart space.

20. As s/he steps in, feel the release, see the shoulders relax, see the little head move up and look the observer in the eyes.

21. You are allowing these fears and worries to be spoken about.

22. As you let fear speak, write down what it says (or record it on your device).

23. See yourself as the observer holding the fear gently and allowing it its say as you keep breathing gently into and out of that space in your body.

24. The act of bringing these fears out into the light by speaking them honors them while also taking away their power to stop you from acting.

25. Some of the most common fears: How will it affect my role in the family? What will my parents think? Can I really do this? What if I alienate my friends? I am not sure I have the skills. Look at what happened the last time I tried something—it was a failure. I dare not. It is safer to stay where I am. At least, I know how to handle these frustrations. I am not sure what I would have to handle if I did what I really would love to do. It is too risky.

26. Stay grounded in your observer as you begin to respond to the fears. Continue to hold the fear gently and breathe with it as you say, "Can you do this slowly, so everyone has a chance to adjust? Are you assuming that someone in your family cannot function without you? Is that a fear? If yes, is that what is stopping their growth?"

27. It is perfectly normal to be afraid to step into something that is not the norm for you or your family and friends. Courage is about feeling the fear and acting anyway. Again, you do not have to do this in one big leap. Ask for guidance to make it a slow and gentle easing into the new way of life. It can be a gentle easing. Also—friends who feel alienated if you step up may not be friends. What if you set the example for them? You learned lessons from the last time you tried something. Take a moment to acknowledge the gift from those lessons. What did you learn? Those lessons are within you and will guide you

now. If you remain afraid and unwilling to take any more risks, that entire experience was wasted. This is time to build trust. Try to put a little toe into the stream of trust. This is clichéd, but there are no rewards without risks. I am here with you. We can do this. Let us start by committing to one small step.

28. Next—as the observer, ask this scared part of you, "What is one small step you can take towards this goal?"
29. Listen for the answer. The scared part of you knows exactly what it is—let the answer and action step emerge
30. Make a note of it and set a date to do it.

10. JOY

Here we are at the tenth meditation. We have worked through a lot of the major "negative" emotions us humans experience over the course of a lifetime. By the time you get here, you have hopefully practiced these meditations enough and have begun to see the impact of spending even a few minutes in that quiet, still space that is at our core.

In preparing to write the vignette for joy, I looked back as I did with each of the other emotions in this book to identify an incident that would exemplify what joy feels like. I realized that although there were very specific events that I remembered in which I felt deep grief or terror or anger, there were many incidents in which I felt joy, peace, connection, and gratitude.

Hardy famously ended *The Mayor of Casterbridge* with the words, "Happiness was but the occasional episode in a general drama of pain." As I come to the end of the book, and reflect on joy, I feel that Hardy had it backwards and the truth is that pain is an occasional episode in the human drama of joy. There are many more instances in my life in which I have been happy and full of joy than I have been sad or fearful.

In his book, *Buddha's Brain: The Practical Neuroscience of Happiness, Love and Wisdom*, Rick Hanson describes how the brain detects negative signals more quickly than signals. Understanding and reacting to threats was fundamental to human survival for centuries, and Hanson explains that our brain evolved to weigh negative events more than positive events. So, we spend a lot of our life immersed in the memory of negative events in the past or anticipating negative events in the future. It is not that you have not had an equal or greater number of positive experiences; it is that the default position of the nervous system is to be primed for disaster.

In part, what these meditations help you to do by reminding you constantly about the peace and quiet that is at your core, and the fact that it is accessible with a few deep breaths and a body scan serves to to reverse this evolutionary bias in favor of focusing on wellbeing, peace and self-acceptance.

After having learned to accept and bring all the parts of you that you rejected or suppressed for most of your life, into your heart, it is now time to amplify the joy. Getting to this meditation and really soaking in the power of it and hopefully learning to act from this space is the ultimate goal of this book and course.

Vignette of joy

An interesting observation as I write this is that even as I intellectually recognize that moments that I have experienced joy far outweigh the moments that I have experienced equivalent grief, I sense my anxiety rising. There is a sense of dread that as I describe these multiple moments of joy, I will somehow attract something bad. My evolutionarily honed habit of bracing for disaster is in full swing. I want to be honest about this to clarify that the work we do on ourselves is the work of a lifetime. As you get used to doing these meditations and become familiar with how your body reacts to various emotions, you become more self-aware, and you will recognize, as I do now, that your nervous system sometimes has a life of its own. Using the skills you have developed through the practice of these meditations, when you become aware of this neurological stress, you will be able to slip into the role of an observer, acknowledge the activation of the nervous system and still continue to do your work. So, having acknowledged my discomfort as I record these moments of joy, let me get on with it.

Images that my mind scrolls through when I think of joy: the gurgling laugh of my six-month-old son as he was thrown up in the air, or watching him, at a little over three years old and two feet high, roar and twist his little body as he pretended to turn into the Incredible Hulk; my young daughter running and throwing her warm arms around my neck as I picked her up from daycare, or hearing that little three-year-old daughter sing, recording her voice for the first time on a cassette tape as she urged me to record, saying, "Press the button, Amma"; watching my son and daughter interact now and seeing the close bond they have as adults; seeing my grandchildren develop into tiny humans with a personality; remembering the time my husband and I were back at the temple where we had been married over three decades ago, feeling connected to him and feeling gratitude at how far we had come and the long road we had traveled; watching a client feel heard and validated for the first time in her life and sensing her appreciation—just a few instances when I experienced pure joy and the accompanying sense of peace and deep gratitude.

As I remember those moments, it is as if I can feel a warm smile start in my heart and spread across my body. My entire body relaxes, and the warmth of the smile is tangible. As I focus on the joy, I can literally feel my energy field open up as I become lighter and looser. I don't feel constricted or tense anywhere. My body feels airy and light, as if I could just float away.

Journal exercise.

Identify the incident in which you remember feeling joyful. You probably have a bunch of incidents like mine, and I would encourage you to make a list. Think about experiences with friends, kids, pets. Think of visiting beautiful places or being out in great weather. Remember when you laughed out loud. You will find that there are innumerable instances when you have been happy. Just this exercise by itself done every day will change how you present yourself to the world.

If you are in a space where you feel unable to bring something up, I invite you to bring to your mind a scene from a book, movie or TV show in which you felt joy vicariously as your favorite character achieved his/her dream. The movie *Little Miss Sunshine*, for example. It is important to take time to find these instances. It is important to show you that regardless of how difficult and exacting your life may have been overall, your life has been peppered, seasoned if you will, with moments when you felt happy.

Write your answers to these questions in the blank space below

Meditation to cultivate joy

Unlike the meditation before this, this meditation is different. The objective here is to soak in the joy and feel it fill every corner of your physical and energetic body. We start with the heart and the space of the observer and go from there.

1. Sit comfortably, with your feet touching the floor.
2. Take a deep breath, feeling the breath fill you up from your lower abdomen all the way to your shoulder blades, and let the breath out with a sigh. Do this step two more times.
3. As your breath comes back to its normal rhythm, I want you to bring to your mind a time in your life when you felt joy. See yourself, smiling and laughing.
4. Now focus on that space just behind your heart—the quiet, still space.
5. Feel a smile start in the quietness. Sense it spreading.
6. A warm, lovely warm feeling moves from your heart space and begins to fill your chest.
7. See and feel the smile and the warmth of it move up your throat, up your face; feel your lips mimic the smile, and feel your eyes crinkle as the smile spreads.
8. Feel the smile move to your abdomen, fill your torso; feel the warmth of the smile move down your legs.
9. Pay attention to what the smile wants you to do. Try moving your body.
10. Sway with the sensation. I invite you to allow your legs to move in a little dance.
11. As this smile fills your body, feel it move out of you and sense this feeling of joy and warmth surrounding you and holding you.
12. As you move your body, feel joy and warmth radiating from you and spreading to others in your immediate vicinity, and eventually, feel this smile that started in your heart spread across the world.
13. Stay in this space for two minutes (count to 120 on your fingers).

14.   Then gently, slowly, bring yourself back into the room.

Thank you. You have come to the end of this set of meditations. Thank you because few people undertake journeys of self-transformation. Thank you because by doing the meditations in this book, you have hopefully learned to be a little bit more accepting, a little bit more compassionate and a little bit more loving towards yourself. As a result, you have increased the acceptance, compassion and love in the world.

Honestly, this is just the beginning. If you would like to know more about how to leverage the work you have done here into creating bigger changes in your life and creating a life you dream about, please contact me at info@freeingourselves.com.

My website:
www.seeta2durga.com